A Gem for a Strand of Pearls

Book # 1

Thank you Clay and Sheila for being such a wonderful friends and for encouraging me to go forward with my book, "A Gem For a Strand of Pearls."

May you be blessed as you find treasures in my songs and poems.

With love and prayers,
Darlene Doyle Hill
7-21-23

A Gem for a Strand of Pearls

Darlene Doyle Hiller

Xulon Press

Xulon Press
2301 Lucien Way #415
Maitland, FL 32751
407.339.4217
www.xulonpress.com

© 2023 by Darlene Doyle Hiller

All rights reserved solely by the author. The author guarantees all contents are original and do not infringe upon the legal rights of any other person or work. No part of this book may be reproduced in any form without the permission of the author.

Due to the changing nature of the Internet, if there are any web addresses, links, or URLs included in this manuscript, these may have been altered and may no longer be accessible. The views and opinions shared in this book belong solely to the author and do not necessarily reflect those of the publisher. The publisher therefore disclaims responsibility for the views or opinions expressed within the work.

Unless otherwise indicated, Scripture quotations taken from the King James Version (KJV) – *public domain*.

Paperback ISBN-13: 978-1-66287-511-3
Ebook ISBN-13: 978-1-66287-512-0

PARTICIPANTS IN THE SAGA OF A GEM FOR A STRAND OF PEARLS

• • • • • • • • • • • • •

DON HILLER - My awesome husband who 'let me be me' and who gifted me with my elegant Mikimoto pearls.

DAVID HILLER - Our oldest son and his wife Beth who gave up everything they had worked so hard for in Massachusetts to move to Florida after Don died so I would not be alone.

DIANE SNIDER - my older sister and mentor and our friend Rita who came with Diane and I on our trip to Boston.

MARJORIE JULIAN - Breeder of Adorabelle Pearl. In her prime she was a famous ballet dancer in New York City. In her retirement she was a breeder of Yorkshire terriers and miniature poodles.

AMALIA - daughter of Marjorie Julian.

BENJAMIN - A ¼ pound Yorkshire terrier puppy bred by Marjorie and who was the major influence in the creation of this wonderful story.

ADORABELLE PEARL, "BELLE" - The star of this saga.

DEDICATION

· · · · · · · · · · ·

Adorabelle Pearl, a precious Yorkshire terrier, was a gift given to me by my heavenly Father to cherish and care for eleven wonderful years. We were seldom apart except for Sundays when I was at church. Those who knew us joked about us being 'attached at the hips'. She helped me to get through many heartaches and sorrows.

IN APPRECIATION
• • • • • • • • • • • • •

I wish to thank my grandson, Daren Hiller whose knowledge and skills on the computer made my project possible. And to thank his fiancé Jessica Winfield, owner/operator of Orange Street Bridal Photography of Brooksville, FL who was so creative with the photos.

To my friend Carolyn Rosemary Sparks without whose encouragement and leadership this book probably would not have come to fruition. Rosemary invited me to her home for a bible study where I shared some of my poems with her and the girls. She appreciated my God-given gift of writing and told me I needed to get my work to a publisher. She 'sparked' my creative embers and I began writing again. And with her encouragement I am in the process of getting a book published. She is a very precious friend whom I love and appreciate. God bless you Rosemary.

I would like to acknowledge my thanks to folks who have been great influences in my life. First of all my loving parents who stressed the importance of honesty and integrity, To my grandmother, Nana Crocker, who loved the Lord and instilled that love into my heart. (See poem in chapter three, "One More Cookie In The Jar"). And my high school English teacher, Ms. Sherwood who taught me the importance of learning proper English grammar. To Mr. Drollett, my Sunday school teacher who brought me to a saving knowledge of the Lord. And to my husband Don who allowed me to be alone with my thoughts. To my sisters, Diane and Denise whose 'words of wisdom' often sparked my creative juices. And most importantly to God, without whose inspiration I could do nothing.

One of my favorite bible verses: Philippians 4:13

"I can do all things through Christ who strengthens me," Amen

God Bless You

FOREWORD

A wonderful, true story of an animal lover, a dog breeder, a precious Yorkshire terrier and one of God's most elegant creations, the pearl.

The pearl was created by an irritant to the oyster, which was harvested and became a part of a strand of pearls and eventually made its way to the show case at Sears. It was lovingly cared for by the sales associate who, in time, purchased it.

This is the beginning of a sometimes sad, yet delightful tale of

<u>"A GEM FOR A STRAND OF PEARLS"</u>.

As an added bonus to my story I have included a collection of informative and enjoyable poems that will warm your heart. These poems were written by me, inspired by God over a period of thirty years or so. May God bless you as you read them.

Darlene Doyle Hiller.

A GEM FOR A STRAND OF PEARLS

• • • • • • • • • • • • • • • •

Only four pounds of flesh, blood and hair,
And adorable as she could be.
This precious little yorkie stood out in a crowd.
That four pounds of love could fill a huge cavity.

She was born on November 11th, 1992,
Weighing in at a quarter of a pound.
Her breeder's name was Marjorie.
As a breeder her reputation was renowned.

I originally met Marjorie at a vets in Beverly, MA.
She was holding Benjamin, a tiny little yorkie.
Being a yorkie lover, I went over and sat beside her.
This meeting was just meant to be.

Benjamin at one week old

Marjorie invited me to her home.
The invitation was too hard to resist.
Although I was very busy packing to move to Florida,
Her invitation was high on my list.

On June of 1993 I went to Marjorie's home.
A little yorkie snuck out and ran to meet me.
The look in her eyes said, "please take me home!"
I knew in my heart that I must set her free.

Breeder Marjorie holding Belle & Benjamin

Marjorie did not want to part with Belle.
She planned to use her to reproduce.
So all I could do was to visit with her,
Praying for her hold on Belle to loose.

I'd been visiting with Belle for several months,
Each time hoping Marjorie would change her mind.
But this day would be different for I had brought with me,
My strand of pearls 'of the finest kind'.

I handed Marjorie the blue, embroidered bag,
Lined with satin to protect the pearls from harm.
She stared in awe and amazement,
As she slowly draped them across her arm.

It was love at first sight when she saw them,
As it was when I first met Belle.
We both agreed and the deal was made.
She would miss her dog I could tell.

Belle was always such a joy,
So adorable in every way.
Her loving, high-spirited demeanor
Could bring peace and joy to my darkest day.

That day came when my husband Don died.
It was on the morning of April 19th, 2004.
But I knew with Jesus' help and Belle by my side,
That God would my peace restore.

In October of 2004 we took a trip up north.
There was friend Rita, sister Diane, Belle and I.
Belle was just the most perfect traveler.
To list her attributes, I could not even try.

On October 26th
While visiting with Diane's family
Belle got really, really sick.
We rushed her to emergency.

An aneurism in her spleen was the diagnosis,
There was nothing the doctors could do.
In just a very few moments
Belle's life on earth would be through.

Only four pounds of flesh, blood and hair.
How could her loss be so great?
She loved me with such an unselfish love.
I know we will meet again at heaven's 'pearly' gate.

This poem was written by Belle's owner Darlene S. Hiller 11/2004. This is the end of Adorabelle Pearl's {Belle's}story, but not the end of the saga of:

"A GEM FOR A STRAND OF PEARLS"

<u>Mikimoto Pearls purchased by author in 1988</u>

PART TWO

A Gem For A Strand Of Pearls
· ·

<u>the rest of the story…</u>

B̲efore moving to Florida in 1993 we lived in Beverly, MA. Don had retired. I was working at Sears in Peabody in the jewelry department. We had a shipment of *Mikimoto pearls* come in. I fell in love with a particular strand. They were the perfect size, color and length for me. They were so elegant. But they surely were not in our budget. So I just took good care of them while they were in the store, hoping no one would buy them.

Then shortly before our twenty-fifth wedding anniversary our manager told us that we were putting all the pearls on sale. I went home and told Don about it. He said to me, "If you want them then get them". He was so good to me.   The next day I went and bought them. With the sale price and my employee discount they were in our budget. I felt so elegant when I wore them.

As life marches on it involves many changes. My husband Don got very sick in 1981. He was forced to sell the business he founded in 1964, Hiller's Auto Body. He took on a job as Building Superintendent at an elderly housing complex.

Don loved his job but was growing tired of the long, cold New England winters. Don loved gardening so we began to make plans to move to sunny Florida.

Don gardening in Florida with dogs Belle & Wendy

I got sick in 1991 and was forced to retire. In 1993 we moved to Spring Hill, FL, just up the street from my sister Denise and her husband Ed. We were so happy, but did miss family back home in MA. So we bought a motor home to make visits easier and more fun. Belle loved traveling in our motor home. We had worked our way up to a 'Class A' motor coach, I would put a pillow on my lap and Belle would sit up there like she 'owned the world'.

After about ten wonderful years in Florida my precious husband Don got sick and passed away. Belle was a lot of comfort to me, but only six months after Don died, my buddy Belle died, as mentioned in the first part of this saga. I was so blessed to have my family, Dave and Beth and their daughter Meagan and Daren, Sr. and Daren, Jr. to help me.

Our home in Spring Hill required a lot of maintenance. My sister Diane, a recent widow, had purchased a home in Brookridge, a manufactured home community in Brooksville,

FL. While helping Diane find a home I found one that I liked and it was just around the corner from her. I prayed about it and it seemed like a good move. That was my first large purchase as a widow. I was kept very busy unpacking boxes etc. But my home was so empty without Don and Belle. I spent a lot of time talking to the Lord.

At this time Dave and Beth, our son and daughter-in-law were still living in Beverly, MA, but were in the process of moving to Florida and changing jobs. Beth was working as a hairdresser at a popular salon in Beverly, MA.

One of the clients was a lady named Amalia, who was the daughter of Marjorie, the breeder of Adorabelle Pearl. Amalia's mom had recently passed away and she was missing her so much. She told Beth she would love to hear a nice story about her. Beth told her she had _just_ that story.

She told her about Belle and how much she was loved and how her Mom and I got to be good friends. And that I paid for Belle with a strand of beautiful *Mikimoto Pearls*. Amalia loved the story. She told Beth that she had those pearls in a safety deposit box. She remembered how much her Mom loved them. Amalia asked Beth if she thought I would like to have those pearls back. Beth told her she knew I would as they were a gift from my husband for our twenty-fifth wedding anniversary. Amalia told Beth she did not care about the pearls so if I wanted them she would sell them to me for $500.00, the price Marjorie would have charge for her yorkie.

I was a recent widow and trying to live within a budget. How could I come up with $500.00? So I did what I usually do when I need wisdom and guidance...I turned to the Lord. I asked Him to help me find a way to get the money for the pearls if it was meant for me to have them.

A few weeks later two gentlemen stopped by my home in Brookridge and were admiring a huge palm tree in my back yard. It was beautiful, but I hated it as I could not trim it myself. They asked me if I might be interested in selling it. I wanted to give him a big hug, but I had to be *cool* about it. I asked him what he would pay me for it. I knew it was an answer to prayer when he said, "How about $500.00? I quickly signed the agreement and the deal was done. Several weeks later they came by with their heavy equipment and removed the tree and replaced it with a cute little tree that I could trim myself. He gave me $500.00. AMEN!

By now Dave and Beth and family were living in Florida. Beth was going back to Beverly, MA for a visit. She met with Amalia and made the swap. Not only were the pearls and matching earrings in the blue, embroidered, satin-lined bag, there was also a small 'thank you' card I had sent to Marjorie for sharing her Adorabelle Pearl with me. There was also the original Sears price tag and the two round Mikimoto tags containing manufacturer's information that were attached to the pearls when I bought them in 1988.

This is a true story written to show people how God can work miracles in our lives if we just trust him. AMEN

PART THREE

"WITH AN EAR TOWARDS GOD"
● ●

SONGS AND POEMS WRITTEN BY

Darlene Doyle Hiller
inspired by God

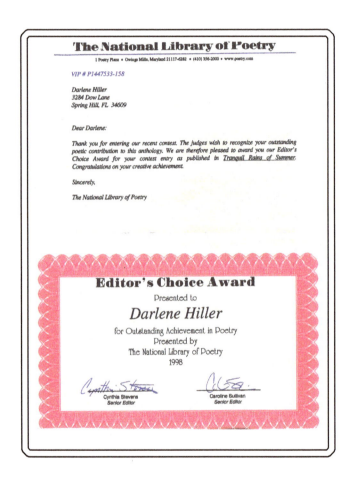

Awarded for Poem "The Pansy"

"THE PANSY"

Have you ever looked into the face of a pansy
Who seemed to be staring right back at you?
Such beauty and perfection in that one little flower,
In its design, in its texture, in its magnificent hue.
I believe that that is God in all of His glory,
The love and praise of His creation overflowing,
His power and might, His gentleness and compassion,
As it wafts and wavers in the gentle breeze that is blowing.
And just like that near-perfect little pansy,
Telling the world of God's love and care,
We too should let God's love from us overflow,
His salvation and glory with others to share.

written by Darlene Doyle Hiller.

This poem won "The Editor's Choice Award" and is in the National Library of Poetry

DAD

• • • •

She gently placed a rose near his tombstone,
As she knelt in the graveyard that day.
She said, "Daddy I love you and miss you so much,
Will I see you in heaven some day?"
You worked so hard for Mom and us kids.
You'd come home so weary and worn.
But you always had time for our tales of woe.
Dad, will I see you when I go home?
Now I don't remember you talking 'bout Jesus.
You enjoyed Sunday mornings alone.
So while Mom and us kids would go to church,
You would do chores at home.
Dad, I know you loved Jesus.
You respected and honored His name,
But did you know Him as your Savior and Lord
When your time for eternity came?
Dad, will I see you in heaven
Singing and playing old hymns?
Sitting around with our family and friends…
Oh Dad will I see you again?
I wish I could know for certain,
Dad that I'd see you again.

written by Darlene Doyle Hiller for my wonderful Dad - 9/13/96

My home was next door to the Masaryktown Baptist Church. I often went early to pray. This day God inspired me to write this song about my Dad. After church I went home and with the help of my mandolin, I put it to music So many folks really liked this song. So in 2005 I submitted it to the ORANGE BLOSSOM COUNTRY MUSIC ASSOCIATION INC. Florida State Songwriting Competition. I was chosen "2005 New Gospel Songwriter of the Year". One of the greatest thrills of my life. AMEN!

THE BIRD

As I was walking through the woods,
I happened to look down.
To see a bird with an injured wing,
Cowering fearfully there on the ground.

So I bent down to pick it up,
Much to its dismay.
How could it know I was there to help,
That it may fly again one day.

At first it resisted with all of its strength,
Biting and screaming and trying to flee.
But finally, too exhausted to fight any longer,
It relaxed and put its faith and trust in me.

I rushed him to a person I knew
Who helps injured birds to fly.
He said it would take a while to heal,
But one day it would soar through the sky.

And just like that injured little bird
Who steadfastly resisted my love and care,
So often we too try to save ourselves,
Rather than trusting Him for our burdens to bear.

Now your troubles may not be a life or death matter.
They may even seem trivial compared to another.
But, if it bothers you…it bothers God.
He wants to help you, your storms to weather.

There is One who is with you through the woods of your life.
One who loves you and knows your pain.
Why don't you allow Him to 'pick you up',
And help you to soar again?

written by Darlene Doyle Hiller - 8/11/02

LAY ASIDE PRIDE

Dear Lord please give me a humble heart,
Remembering that all of my blessings come from You.
Even as I was being knit together in my mother's womb,
You were laying out a plan as my body, mind and soul grew.

You gave me a wonderful, loving family
Who taught me to care for fellow man,
And how important it was to read and obey God's word,
And to share His plan of salvation as often as I can.

May I never let pride come forth from my lips,
As I seek to walk *'the narrow way'*,
And let all praise and glory go to you, oh Lord,
Today and every day. Amen!

written to myself, for myself as God spoke to my heart
6/13/ 22 - Darlene Doyle Hiller

BEFORE YOU KNOW IT

Time, time, elusive time,
Time oh where does it go?
Time, time precious time.
Are you making the most of your time here below?

Before you know it you are walking and your talking.
Before you know it you are on your way to school.
Before you know it you are graduating college,
Ready now to face a world that's cold and cruel.

When your young you are sure you'll live forever,
Fame and fortune are the goals for which you strive.
But the years have a way of passing quickly.
Now you're thankful just to be alive.

Along the way did you get to know the Savior?
Along the way did you trust Him as your Lord?
Along the way did you come to Him in prayer?
Along the way did you take time to read His word?

Can you say with the saints that you've a home in heaven,
Prepared by the Savior who bore your sin and shame?.
Along the way did you plan for eternity?
Because, before you know it death could call your name.

written by Darlene Doyle Hiller - inspired by God

CLOTHED IN RIGHTEOUSNESS

For so long I had lived as if I'd live forever,
With no concern for my sin-sick soul.
I was trying to solve all my problems alone.
Self-preservation was my desire, my goal.

Then one day I met the Savior.
My sinful life was stripped away.
I was clothed in the righteousness of Christ my Lord.
Oh praise God, this is where I want to stay.

When I came to the Savior with a repentant heart,
And a desire to love and serve Him,
I was filled with all the goodness of the Godhead bodily,
Clothed in His righteousness, filled to the brim.

This is not to say that I won't stumble or fall,
Or that satan won't have his way.
But I know that when my 'garment' starts coming apart,
I can get down on my knees and to my Savior pray.

And like a sheep that has wandered away from the flock,
He will welcome me back to the fold.
Renewed, refreshed and forgiven by Him.
Clothed in His righteousness, blessings untold.

written by Darlene Doyle Hiller
inspired by God - 5/25/98

CHECK YOUR OIL

Is their oil in your lamp,
Or is it running low?
When the bride groom comes,
Will you be ready to go?

We know not when that time will be,
At noon or dark of night.
So be sure that when you trim your lamp,
The fire will burn bright.

Check your oil, who rules your heart and mind?
Check your oil, to the unlovely are you kind?
Does Jesus Christ live in your heart, of all your plans is
He a part?
Has He cleansed you from all your sins, is your heart's desire
new souls to win?

Check your oil, Christ could come any day.
Check your oil, He may be on His way.
Yes, check your oil, today may be the day.
Yes, today may be THE day.

written by Darlene Doyle Hiller - 6/96
inspired by Matthew 25:1-13

BECAUSE OF LOVE

Darlene's Testimony

Because of love I share my thoughts with you.
How God has blessed my life, as He wants to do for you.

I went to a "Billy Graham Crusade', it was July of '58.
The preacher asked if we knew for sure that if we were to die, would we enter heaven's gate.

Well he got me to thinking about my life and the hereafter.
And about God's plan of salvation, referring to the bible, book, verse and chapter.

Now if the bible were true, as I believed it to be, then I knew I was not prepared for the Savior to see.
So I answered the call to come forward to hear God's plan of salvation He had prepared for me.

I asked the Lord to forgive me for my sins and to come into my heart.
And from that time on I knew that in all I did Christ would be a part.

Because of love Christ walks with me, every day of my life… because of Calvary.
AMEN

written by Darlene Doyle Hiller - 5/28/00

ARE YOU READY FOR THE BATTLE?

Are you ready for the battle, is your armor in its place?
Are you prepared to meet your foe, To meet him squarely face to face?
God tells us in His holy word that we must be prepared at any time to go to war with our equipment all 'four-squared'.

He fights not with a gun or sword, or weapons that we can see.
His target is the hearts and minds of folks like you and me.
So don't wait another minute to put your helmet on.
The helmet of salvation furnished by the grace of God.

It is free and indestructible and guaranteed to fit.
For a soldier in God's army it is a prerequisite.
You'll need righteousness as a breastplate with the 'belt of truth' cinched tight
and feet that are shod with running shoes to speed you on your flight.

To bring the 'Gospel of Good News'
to those who've never heard,
and to those who have not read about it
in His holy word.

To protect you from the fiery darts spewed from the wicked one, you'll need a shield, what better shield than faith in God's own Son. Faith in a God who loves and cares about each and everyone. Oh, we're ready Lord, we're ready now to watch the devil run. Yes, we're ready Lord. we're ready now to watch the devil run! AMEN!

written by Darlene Doyle Hiller - 10/89 inspired by Ephesians 6:10-17

A MOTHER'S HEART

A mother's heart is such a fragile thing,
It takes so very little to make her glad heart sing.
And that very same heart can be broken in two,
By a forgotten 'Special Day', or a hurting word from you.

Mother's child how long has it been since she heard you say, "*I love you!*"?
Have you thanked her for selfless love?
When it came to her child only her best would do.

Why don't you take time to phone her today,
Just to say "Hi Mom, I miss you."
Or maybe recall a pleasant thought from the past.
For you know you will always be her 'baby' what ever you do.

A Mother's heart is so precious indeed.
Who else could love you as she?
She would give her life for her precious child,
As Christ gave His life for you and me.

Written by Darlene Doyle Hiller 1/25/97

A GRANDPARENT'S PRAYER

We lift up our children today to you Lord,
And all of our children's children.
We commit them into your loving arms.
There is no greater gift we could give to them.

You know how precious they are to us Lord,
For you loved your only son too.
Oh, how can we thank you for your sacrifice?
Heartache and pain are so real to you.

So we lift up our children to our Heavenly Father,
As well as their children too.
We can know that whatever befalls them this day,
Was allowed by you.

written by Darlene 'Grammy' Doyle Hiller
8/3/97 - inspired by God

FREE STUFF

When was the last time
You heard the morning birds sing?
When you woke up praising God
For the new day He would bring?

When you noticed, *really* noticed
The flowers being pollinated by the bees?
Or the cows in the pasture
Grazing beneath the huge live oak trees?

God gives us so much 'free stuff'
For our senses to enjoy.
We only need to look about us
To see that nature itself is an awesome 'toy'.

Entertainment doesn't have to be a spectacular event
Performed on a Broadway stage.
God's 'free things' are available for all to see.
They can entertain and intrigue just any age.

For example, have you ever watched a 'dung' beetle
Moving refuge many times her own weight?
The refuge will provide food and warmth for her young.
God's cycle of nature, He is so great!

This poem could just go on and on,
Parading examples of 'free stuff' to see.
It is there for the taking if you have the time.
Appreciation of nature, what a wonderful gift to give to your family.

*If we don't love and appreciate God's
creation, how can we understand the
mind and character of God?*

*God is our highest standard by which
all else is measured.
He is one of whom no greater can be conceived.*

written by Darlene Doyle Hiller - 12/31/00

Dedicated to my brother-in-law, David Hirsh, (Returning Moon) a native American Indian of the Wampanoag Tribe of Cape Cod, MA

David Hirsh with with Diane

EXPECT A MIRACLE

Just plant your tiny seed in the soil of God's greatness,
Then watch it grow, yes watch it grow.
Water it daily with your heart-felt prayers,
Then watch it grow, yes, watch it grow.

Oh, it only takes a speck of faith in a mighty God
For a miracle to happen if you believe, if you only believe.
Ask God for the impossible in faith believing.
Ask for a miracle, then watch for it to happen.

God raised Lazarus from the dead, He turned the water into wine.
Yes, miracles do happen, praise God they still do happen.
He is the same today as He was way back then.
Miracles do happen, oh yes, they still do happen.

Just plant your tiny seed in the soil of God's greatness,
Then watch it grow, yes, watch it grow.
Water it daily with your heart-felt prayers,
Then watch it grow, yes, EXPECT A MIRACLE.

Written by Darlene Hiller - 12/95

ETERNITY

● ● ● ● ● ● ● ●

We need not fear the unknowns of death,
No, there's no need to be afraid.
For our future is in the hands of God,
If our all on His altar's been laid.

We can look right past our darkest hour,
And see a glorious dawn
Illuminated by, "The Bright and Morning Star",
God's promise for sinners reborn.

Yes, child of God, there is no need to weep,
For we'll not make that walk alone.
God has prepared a table before us.
He'll lead us to our new home.

We'll walk and talk and reminisce,
We'll laugh and dance and sing.
We'll praise and worship with the saints of old,
We'll be with the King of Kings. AMEN!

written by Darlene Doyle Hiller - 8/96
inspired by 2nd Corinthians 5:1-8

GOD'S WILL

Lord, I want to do your will today.
I want to walk the narrow way.
May everything I do or say,
Be according to your will.

Lord, oh may I use my eyes to see,
The pain, the hunger, poverty,
Of those less fortunate than me
Who cannot help themselves.

Lord, please use my ears that I might hear,
The cries for help, both far and near,
Of the hungry, food, of the lonely, cheer,
In this world we call our home.

Lord, please use my mouth to share your word,
With unsaved souls who've never heard
About your love, your care, the cross.
Yes, burden my soul for the lost.

Lord, may I do your will today,
May I walk the narrow way.
May everything I do or say,
Be according to your will.

written by Darlene Doyle Hiller - 1993.

DON'T FRET
· · · · · · · · · ·

Don't fret about the past, for it has all been written.
And don't waste time on things you cannot change.
If you really want to know the joy of the Lord,
Then stop trying the past to rearrange.

And don't worry about tomorrow, for it will happen anyway.
Just walk with God, trusting Him as you go.
Remember that His 'on star' button is always 'on'.
He is ready and waiting, His plan for you to show.

Now, free from worry because you're trusting the Lord,
You can concentrate on 'today'.
Expending all your energies on the tasks at hand,
Whether work or school or play.

written by Darlene Doyle Hiller
10/22/00

CIRCLE OF LIFE

When your circle of life is completed
Where will that circle end?

Sometimes that circle seems so large,
Or sometimes so very small.
But always our lives come full circle,
Because of Adam's fall.

God has a home prepared for us,
More glorious than man can know,
If we've trusted in Jesus as our Savior and Lord
That is where we will go.

God knows where you are in your circle of life,
And He knows when and where it will end.
He wants so much to walk hand in hand with you,
Yes, He wants to be your best friend.

When your circle of life is completed,
Where will that circle end?

written by Darlene Doyle Hiller
12/12/97

IN HIS BLOOD

I don't need no washing machine to make sure my robe is clean,
For it's been washed in the blood of Jesus.
No, I don't need no bleach or 'Tide' if in my Savior I abide.
For I've been washed in the blood of Jesus.
In His blood, His cleansing blood,
Yes, I've been washed in the blood of Jesus.

Whether I see Him when I die,
Or go to meet Him in the sky,
I will wear the robe my Savior washed for me.
For it was on that hill called Calvary
That Jesus bled and died for me,
His precious, cleansing blood is all I need.

In His blood, His cleansing blood.
Have you been washed in the blood of Jesus?
In His blood, His cleansing blood.
Oh, praise God I've been washed
In the blood of Jesus.
Yes, I've been washed in the blood of Jesus. AMEN!

written by Darlene Doyle Hiller

A GRANDMOTHER'S HEART

Mothers as you grow older,
And your kids have kids of their own,
You'll find that your heart has made changes,
As you have matured and grown.

When you were young and rearing your kids,
Your heart was tough and strong.
You could take a stand and not be moved
In order to teach your kids right from wrong.

But as you matured your heart seemed to change,
It took on a different design.
All those sharp corners were worn away,
You became more patient, long-suffering - refined.

One of the hardest jobs for a grandmother to do,
Is to raise grandkids as their own.
To take a heart that has become worn and stretched with time,
And make it tough again 'til the grandkids are grown.

So kids don't forget her heart
That has become worn soft and smooth
From years of loving and giving unselfishly,
Surely could use a refill, don't you agree?

written by Darlene Doyle Hiller - 3/4/98
dedicated to my sister Diane

Darlene with her sister Diane

GET UP AND GET GOING

Happy in Jesus, oh how can it be?
With joy in my heart, just Jesus and me.
He has plans for my life that I can't even imagine.
He says, "Darlene, get busy, it is time now to begin"!

Don't tell me about your age, aches and pains,
You've told me about them time and time again.
Think about my love and care for you,
About all the heartaches I helped you get through.

Put on the armor of God so we can lay out a plan.
To complete your dreams while helping your fellow man.
Take all those wishes floating around in your heart,
Make them real and today is a good day to start.

written by Darlene Doyle Hiller
inspired by Philippians 4:13

"I can do all things through Christ which strengthens me."
Philippians 4:13

HE'S COMING BACK

Jesus Christ is coming back,
He's coming back I know.
I'm assured of His appearing
For the bible tells me so.

It will only take a moment,
Just the twinkling of an eye,
And I will meet my Savior
Who will take me home on high.

We will be joined by all the saints of old
Who died so long ago,
And by our friends and family
If the Savior they did know.

Have you come to Jesus Christ the Lord
With a repentant heart?
Have you asked Him to forgive you for your sins
And for your life to be a part?

God wants to fill your heart with love,
And a peace that you've never known.
He wants for you to know for certain
That heaven will be your eternal home.

For Jesus Christ is coming back,
Yes, He's coming back I know..
I'm assured of His appearing
For the bible tells me so.

written by Darlene Doyle Hiller - 4/25/98
inspired by 1 Thessalonians 4:13-18

I JUST COULDN'T IMAGINE LIFE WITHOUT YOU LORD

I just couldn't imagine life without you Jesus.
Oh, I just couldn't imagine life without you Lord.
You're the Lily of the Valley, your everything to me,
And I just couldn't imagine life without you Lord.

Now when the day is dawning I come to you in prayer.
I read your word and meditate, I know that you are there,
And I just couldn't imagine life without you Jesus,
No, I just couldn't imagine life without you Lord.

And as I travel through the day and troubles come my way,
I know that you will see me through, my Comfort and my Stay,
And I just couldn't imagine life without you Jesus,
No, I just couldn't imagine life without Lord.

It's getting dark, it's evening now and as I look back on this day
Of things I did or didn't do, that I did or didn't say,
And I just couldn't imagine life without Jesus.
No I just couldn't imagine life without you Lord.

I just couldn't imagine death without Lord.
I just couldn't imagine dying all alone.
Heaven's just as real to me as your death on Calvary,

And I just couldn't image life without you Jesus,

Oh, I just couldn't imagine life without you Lord. Amen.

written by Darlene Doyle Hiller -- 1990

It is my testimony song

HAPPY MOTHER'S DAY

I'm expecting so much, it's Mother's Day.
And I have children you know.
Will they take the time to remember me
With flowers and gifts, their love to show?

But wait! Maybe this year, instead of looking to them
For gifts of love and appreciation,
I think I will be the one to take the time
To thank them for their creation.

For without my children I would not be a "Mother",
With a heart full of memories to ponder.
Memories of 'first times', of struggles and laughter.
Yes, through the garden of memories I just love to wander.

So this year kids it is my turn to give thanks
For the privilege of being your "MOM".
For motherhood is the fulfillment of a young girl's dream.
The dream of marriage, kids and a God-honored home.

Written with a heart full of love for my two sons,
David and Daren
by their Mom, Darlene Hiller 5/97

David and Daren Hiller

GOD THE FATHER

God, we have something in common.
In one way I'm not so different from you.
I have someone that I love very dearly,
Yes, I have a son just like you.

But, your son was born in a manger.
No doctors or nurses were there.
No choice of which outfit to where that day,
No rattles, no toys and no rocking chair.

No family gathered 'round to admire
This beautiful newborn babe,
Or to give a comforting word to his mother,
Who lay nearby in a bed made of hay,

God, you loved your son with all of your heart,
Just the same as I.
But my son was born with hopes and plans,
While your son was born to die.

Oh thank you God for so great a love,
You gave the very best that you had.
May I never forget that the creator of all
Was also a loving Dad. AMEN!

written by Darlene Doyle Hiller 8/95
thinking of our son David

GOD ALONE

Is your heart weighed down with anxious thoughts?
God tells us that in everything to rejoice.
So even now reach out to Him
As you seek His comforting voice.

The peace of God will fill your heart,
Surpassing all you've ever known.
It is God alone who can do this.
Yes, no one else but God alone.

So rejoice and praise His name
As you walk through life today.
Yes, sing aloud to your Savior, for He is
THE TRUTH THAT LIGHTS OUR WAY.

written by Darlene D. Hiller,
inspired by Philippines 4:4-9

OUR LEGACY

What legacy will you leave to your children,
And to your children's children?
Will it be one that they will be proud to share,
Or a book that no one will open?

Life is not a dress rehearsal,
We have only one chance to 'get it right'.
So make your life choices wisely,
Using God's word as your source of light.

One day you are just an innocent child,
Your thoughts and plans so contemporary.
And then before you know it you are all grown up.
That child is now just a memory.

Have you accomplished all that you had hoped for in life?
Are you where you want to be?
As you examine your life are there things you would change?
To that question most would answer ;YES!;, don't you agree?

I believe a good formula for happiness would be
To strive to be the very best that you can.
And while taking care of your wants and needs,
Take time to reach out to help your fellow man.

God created us in the image of Him,
With body, mind and soul.
But each one of these entities needs to be fed
If true and lasting happiness is your goal. AMEN!

written by Darlene Doyle Hiller
inspired by God

LIGHT UP YOUR CANDLE

The winds of war are raging,
It seems the Son of liberty has set.
There's corruption all around us,
But don't give up, there's still hope yet.

Just light up your candle
In this world of dark despair.
Light up your candle,
You'll find there's light to share.

There's so much pain and suffering
You don't know where to start.
God said to start with one lost soul,
To ease one aching heart.

A kindly word to a hurting soul,
A deed done out of love.
A monetary helping hand
Known just to you and God above.

It only takes a little spark
To start a raging fire.
A fire fanned by loving, giving,
Praying for His power.

Your one small light could start a chain
Of love spread 'round the world.
Of people helping people,
The flag of peace unfurled.
Yes, light up your candle,

In this world of dark despair.
Light up your candle
You'll find there's light to spare.

written by Darlene Doyle Hiller - 1989
inspired by God

KEEP ETERNITY'S VALUES IN VIEW

Keep eternity's values in view, my child
Yes, eternity's values in view.
Don't concern yourself with worldly things,
Seek God's guidance for what you should do.

Sing and shout and praise the Lord,
Giving thanks to Him for all He has done,
For family and for heartfelt friends,
And for the struggles He has helped you to overcome.

Then just keep singing and shouting AMEN!!! AMEN!!!
Sing it until JOY fills your soul.
Sing it with eternity's values in view,
And winning hearts for Jesus is your goal.

written by Darlene Doyle Hiller - 5/26/22
dedicated to my wonderful friend Evelyn

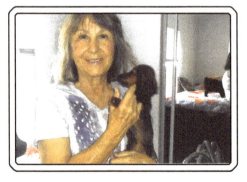

My friend Evelyn with her dog Hope

LORD, I WANT TO DO YOUR WILL TODAY

• • • • • • • • •

Lord, I want to do your will today,
I want to walk the narrow way.
May everything I do or say,
Be according to your will.

Lord, oh may I use my eyes to see,
The pain, the hunger, poverty
Of those less fortunate than me.
Who cannot help themselves.

Lord, please use my ears that I might hear,
The cries for help both far and near.
Of the hungry, food, of the lonely, cheer,
In this world we call our home.

Lord, please use my mouth to share your word,
With unsaved folks who've never heard,
About your love, your care, the cross.
Yes, burden my soul for the lost.

Lord, may I do your will today,
May I walk the narrow way,
May everything I do or say,
Be according to your will.

written by Darlene Doyle Hiller
inspired by my desire to serve Him

OUR GRANDDAUGHTER MEAGAN

Meagan is so beautiful, so innocent
Playing joyfully in the tree.
Her body draped across the limbs,
So young and so carefree.

Now she's hanging upside-down,
Her hair flowing in the breeze.
"Oh Lord, please take good care of her."
"Hey Grammy, take my picture please."

With a twirl and a flip of her body
She is back down on the ground,
Running through the thick, green grass,
Doing cartwheels 'round and 'round.

Meagan's giggles attracted some neighbor girls
Who soon would join her in her play.
Oh thank you Lord for our Meagan.
I feel so blessed today.

written by Darlene "Grammy" Hiller
4/25/98

Meagan Hiller

DO YOU KNOW...FOR SURE?

May I ask you a question
Of utmost important to you?
Today if death should call your name,
Would heaven's gate you walk through?

In the book of Romans,
Verse 13 of chapter 10
God assures us of salvation
If we've been born again

Go back to verses 9 and 10
In chapter 10 of Romans.
You'll find God's salvation plan,
His gift to lost and dying man.

Just confess your sins to Jesus,
Ask Him now to be your Lord.
Then give your heart and soul to Him,
Take time to read His word.

Now you know *for sure*
That you're a blood-bought child of God,
As promised in His holy word.
For His death on Calvary paid the price for you and me.

"For everyone who calls on the name of the Lord <u>will</u> be saved."

Romans 10:13

"If you confess with your mouth that Jesus is Lord, and believe in your heart that God raised Him from the dead you <u>will</u> be saved.

Romans 10:9,10

DO NOT DELAY FOR *NO CHOICE* IS
A CHOICE THAT YOU'VE MADE A FTER ALL,

written by Darlene Doyle Hiller - 2/22/05
inspired by God's word

WHO LOVES YOU MOST OF ALL?

• • • • • • • • • • •

There are so many kids in this world today,
How can God watch over them all?
Does He know when they're hurt, or scared or cold?
Does He care when the slip and fall?

God tells us that kids are most special to Him.
He loves them with all of His heart.
He knows everything about every kid.
He's known them from the start.

He knows the things they like to do,
And He knows the things they hate.
He knows when it's time to answer their prayers,
And He knows when it's better to wait,

Yes, God knows about you and how special you are.
And He loves to hear you sing 'Jesus' songs.
He loves it when you come to Him in prayer.
And when your heart to Him belongs.

So ask Jesus today to come into your heart,
And to be your Savior and Lord.
Tell Him you're sorry for the things you've done wrong.

And begin today to take time to read His word.

Yes, Jesus loves YOU most of all,
You are so precious to Him.
He loves to hear you laugh and play.
Yes, Jesus is your very best friend.

written by Darlene Doyle "Grammie" Hiller - 2/17/1996
for my grandson Daren, Jr.

Daren Hiller Jr.

VETERAN'S DAY

Today is a day set aside to remember
Those who served in the Armed Forces so faithfully.
Many were maimed, or even gave of their lives,
That we as a nation might remain strong and free.

It is hard to imagine the "hell" of war
When you've never been involved first-hand.
The soldiers who were fortunate to come back home alive,
Surely brought with them nightmares of war in a foreign land.

I stand in awe for those who fought for our freedom.
Many held captive by oppressive, Godless tyrants,
Tortured and beaten, starved and enslaved.
In God's book of heroes these are the giants.

Memorial Day is more than just a day off from work,
Time spent with our friends and family.
Let's take time today to remember our heroes of old.
And pray for those now serving in America's military.

written by Darlene Doyle Hiller - 5/29/00
Dedicated to my hero, my second cousin,
Charles H. Doyle, 509th Parachute Infantry, WWII

Charles H Doyle

THROUGH THE EYES OF THE KING

As you look around at the world today,
At the poverty and despair,
The helpless, the homeless, the abused,
With crime rampart everywhere,

Do you look away in anger wondering,
"Why doesn't *someone* do *something*?"
Or do you see the great needs of the hurting world
Through the eyes of the King?

Through His eyes, through His eyes, through the eyes of Jesus.
Compassion and love from the Father above,
That's what the world needs my friend
Caring and loving, humbly giving, a helping hand to lend.

We need to reach out in love as our Savior did
Two thousand years ago.
When Jesus suffered and died so that we might live.
Oh how He loved us so.

So take time today with Jesus to pray
And ask to see the world through His eyes.
For we can be that *someone* who does *something*,
If we would just see the world through His eyes.
Yes, through His eyes, through His eyes, through the
eyes of Jesus.

written by Darlene Doyle Hiller

THE HEART OF GOD

The heart of God, the infinite heart of God,
Has been pounding since before time began.
It is fueled by the blood, His precious blood,
The blood that was shed for sinful man.

The heart of God is the epitome of compassion.
His hand of forgiveness reaching out for all to grasp.
Encompassing even the vilest of sinners.
This forgiveness is free. you just have to ask.

There is no fence so high that God's love cannot scale it.,
And no wall so thick that His love cannot break through..
The love in God's heart is not like the world has to offer.
It is immutable. omnipresent, and it is altogether true.

Oh, I think about the heart of God,
How massive it must be.
For while loving and caring for the rest of the world,
He can still love and care for me.

written by Darlene Doyle Hiller
inspired by God 4/30/97

Sometimes We Have to Fall

Is your life like Humpty Dumpty's, is it cracked and broken apart?
Your heart's desire is restoration, but you don't know where to start.

It seems that not so long ago you sat proudly on that wall,
A nearly perfect 'egg shaped' life, you never thought that you could fall.

Then the winds of life blew up a storm and you were blown right off that wall..
And all the king's horses and all the king's men couldn't save you from that fall.

For it seems sometimes we have to fall to know that God is what we need.
He will mend our broken, shattered lives if to His word we heed.

The one who created this universe also created man.
There is no one too hopeless or lost to God.
The world cannot save us
But the King of Kings can,

So when life is hard and times are tough,
And your future's uncertain indeed,
Fear not for sometimes we have to fall,
To find that God is what we need.

Healer, provider, sustainer and friend.
Yes, Christ is all we need.

written by Darlene Doyle Hiller - inspired by God

PERFECT FOR GOD'S EARS

When we come to the Savior with our burdens and praise,
When we pour out our hearts to the Lord,
There's no need to worry if the words aren't just 'right',
For Jesus takes our prayers to God.

We can concentrate on our worship and praise,
On loving and adoring our Savior,
On our prayers for those we know are in need,
Seeking forgiveness for our sinful behavior.

As our prayers wend their way to our Father in heaven.
Our prayers of hope, needs and fears,
Jesus will take our heartfelt prayers,
And make them perfect for God's ears.

Yes, He'll make them perfect for God's ears. AMEN!

written by Darlene Doyle Hiller - 2/18/96

ONE MORE COOKIE IN THE JAR

When I was just a little girl
To Nana's house I'd go.
She loved to share her cooking secrets
She thought I ought to know.

She would let me make an awful mess
While making puffs we filled with cream.
Then she would tell me, "Honey, just remember,
To scrape your mixing bowl clean."

When our 'creations' were complete
We'd enjoy them with our tea.
Then Nana would talk about Jesus,
And how dearly He loved me.

I asked her why she talked about Him,
For heaven seems so very far.
She said, "It's like scraping the sides of the mixing bowl,
One more cookie in the jar."

One more child to love the Savior,
Who, one day, Jesus Christ will see.
One more precious soul in heaven
Where they will spend eternity.

One more soul in heaven...
One more cookie to share.
One more child to serve the Savior...
One who will know the power of prayer.

written by Darlene Doyle Hiller - dedicated to Nana Crocker

Nana Crocker

MAY I LOVE THEM ENOUGH

Oh thank you Lord for my family and friends,
And the folks I've yet to meet.
May I love them enough to tell them about you,
And that without you their lives are incomplete.

Yes, may I care enough to tell them 'bout Jesus,
Of His love and His saving grace.
To tell them about God's perfect plan of salvation.
And that 'hell' is a very real place.

For today could be the day that they meet the Savior,
To give account of their lives here on earth.
All the good deeds they've done are not important to Him,
He'll simply ask if they've trusted in Him and believed in His incarnate birth.

For death is a fate each one of us faces,
We will all stand before God's judgment seat.
Will they be able to say "I'm saved by God's grace.",
Or will they go to 'hell' in defeat?

There is no one here on earth that can pray them into heaven,
That can cleanse their sins or forgive their burdened soul.
They must go to God themselves for forgiveness and salvation
If heaven is their eternal goal.

It doesn't take wealth or a great education to be part of
God's family.
Just ask for forgiveness and believe in the Savior.
How much easier could it be?

Oh Lord may I love them enough to tell them
About you and what you've done for me.
May I never tire of praying for them,
Until I see you in eternity.

written by Darlene Doyle Hiller - inspired by God - 10/95

THE MANATEE

We got to swim with a manatee
In a spring-fed river in Weeki Wachee.
The sheriff came by to tell us, "Don't touch!".
"This is their space, please give them that much."

These gentle giants are so large,
That an adult would barely fit into a one-car garage.
These wonderful mammals are peaceful and serene.
They are herbivores, eating only nature's green

Their only enemy is man and his greed.
With pollution, boat props and the need for speed.
We must start NOW to protect the marvelous manatee,
Or the next generation may not have any to see.

written by Darlene Doyle Hiller